M000202189

Brand New Me: The Pursuit of Wholeness
Journey from Pain to Greatness

Chautè Thompson, LMHC, CDWF
Foreword by Natolie Warren, LPC

Brand New Me: The Pursuit of Wholeness

Copyright © by Chautè Thompson. All rights reserved.

Published by Chautè Thompson, Brand New Me, LLC
Brandnewmejourney.com

Cover Design
Brand It Beautifully™
Branditbeautifully.com

Editing
Anissa Sonia

This Book is Dedicated to:

Women:

Women in a strained relationship, experiencing the internal struggle of desiring something different than what she is currently experiencing.

Women who are no longer in strained relationships but have lost themselves and are unsure of what tomorrow can bring.

Women who have journeyed through the beginning, middle and are currently lifelong learners of their experiences.

Men

Men who have experienced strained relationships and would like to journey to wholehearted living.

Men who want to get a glimpse into the hearts of some women to aid them in being more empathetic to the journey she might have endured.

ANYONE who wants to live *authentically* <u>comfortable</u> in the skin they are in!

TABLE OF CONTENTS

Foreword

Your life experiences up until this very moment have shaped you into the person you are today. These experiences tell a story of your life that either empowered you or stripped you of your identity, worth and security or revealed those same things to you. If you are not careful, your negative experiences can be internalized and keep you in a state of brokenness and suffering. However, you do not have to live in suffering. You can break the hold of brokenness and live in a state of completion and wholeness.

In this book, *Brand New Me: The Pursuit of Wholeness*, you will go on an emotional journey with some courageous women who share the raw truth of their stories of healing and hope. The women encourage us to break free and not stay in the state of brokenness. Each story demonstrates the power of self-healing tools to include letting go, self-forgiveness, and seeking support. Their stories show the paralyzing power of fear and the liberating power of courage. The authenticity and vulnerability of the stories you will read will not only capture your attention, they will also free your soul. By reading this book, you will gain the hope to activate your inner power of choice. Further, the stories demonstrate that you can affect change in your life, no matter what decisions you have previously made.

As a psychotherapist and transformational coach, I support women walk in a state of completion and wholeness, learn to heal themselves and teach them how to be the best version of themselves. I could say that my master's degree in Counseling and my master's degree in Clinical Psychology along with fourteen years in the field make me an expert in the topic of wholeness. However, my own personal self-discovery and inner work on awakening my state of wholeness has taught me more and stretched me further than my educational background. My own personal experiences speak to the power of knowing your worth. I too did not know my own worth which resulted in me not living in the fullest expression of myself, making irrational life decisions, connecting myself with individuals who could not appreciate my value and settling for less than what I really wanted. Because of wanting more in life, I went down my own journey of self-discovery and I love the whole woman that I have become.

From my perspective, wholeness is about waking up to who you truly are. It is a state of being. In order to walk into this state of wholeness, you have to remove the barriers and blocks that hinder your ability to see your wholeness. It is not something that is given to you, it is something that is already within you. When you walk in wholeness, you make peace with the past and the present. In this book, you get the opportunity to see this process unfold in each of the ladies' stories and how it shifts then into wholeness.

Chautè Thompson is a colleague who shares a similar passion in supporting women restore their self-worth and I highly respect the work that she does. She desires for women to move from brokenness to wholeness. Chautè knows all too well the need to move from brokenness to wholeness from her own journey as well as the countless individuals she has walked with in therapy. We both know the importance of this work to have emotional stability, healthy relationships and to live full lives.

Therefore, I am highly delighted to recommend that you read this book because we all have a story and are on a journey of discovering ourselves. This book will support you walk courageous in your authentic truth, even as far as assisting you make those hard life decisions to choose wholeness over brokenness. No matter what you have experienced in life, you too can awaken your state of wholeness. You are not broken, there are just parts of you that you have not discovered. I challenge you to give yourself permission to show up whole every day. At the core of who you are, whether you feel like it right now, you are a whole woman. It is time that you embrace wholeness that is available to us all.

By Natolie Warren, LPC

Founder of **InPowerment**
and *The Whole Woman Experience*

Trapped

When is the last time you felt trapped?

Trapped in the movie of your life

In the reruns of heartbreak

No matter how much you fight—

Trapped!

When is the last time you lived in a bubble?

The bubble of hope

Light at the end of the tunnel

Only to find more twists and turns the further in you travel.

When is the last time you ran out of tears?

Sad but can't express

Tired of hearing yourself sing another sad song

Does anyone see it in your eyes?

In your smile?

In the phrases you choose to say?

Are you being heard?

Or are you trapped, taking up space?

SAVE YOURSELF.

-Chautè Thompson

Enough

Chanel Spencer

I stared at the blood dripping from my split lip, filling my cupped hands as the words he had just said echoed in my mind and imprinted on my soul. My lip was throbbing from the impact of his fist that he had used as a weapon to put me back in my place. The physical pain was real, but the real pain was hidden deep within. Years of hurt and emotions were buried under the masks where I hide. Behind those masks were the shame, pain, and misery that I wore like my own skin. I was reluctantly traveling down a path I no longer recognized, with destruction as my guide. Darkness engulfed every ounce of light until I could no longer recognize the girl I once was, one filled with light, hope, and love. I believed every word that he said about me. His words seemed to give value and confirm every negative thought I had about myself. I allowed his words to become my truth. Ugly. Unlovable. Worthless. Tainted. Embarrassment. Disgusting. Disappointment. Failure.

Weak. I gave into the hurt and pain, allowing it to swallow me whole claiming me as its victim.

For a brief moment I just stood there, cold, alone, and numb from the pain. Every drop of blood seeping from my lip represented a dream that I longed to find again. I stood in the mirror staring at my visible wounds. Wounds that represented what had been going on inside me for years. While in that mirror, began to remember who I was and connected with the light that once held my dreams. However, the fear still consumed me. As I stared at my reflection trying to figure out a way to repair my lip and cover up the fresh bruises, I wondered if this would ever end. Fear was the warden who held me prisoner. My fear bonded me to the toxic relationships that consumed me. Fear for my life. Fear for my safety. Fear of being alone and unloved. I constantly found myself walking on eggshells. Always afraid that I would do or say the wrong thing. Fear was my normal. It was my friend, my best friend. As my closest confidant, I trusted fear and allowed it to control how I made life decisions. Looking back, there was never really a time that I felt safe, secure, and protected.

When I met this man he represented the security that I so desperately needed. I was instantly attracted to him, everyone loved him, all the women swooned over him which made me feel valuable. He was the ideal boyfriend on the exterior. The day he decided he wanted to be with me felt so unreal. I couldn't believe that someone like him would choose someone like me. He seemed to be everything I ever dreamed about and more. All of the fear I felt turned into false security and superficial love. He seemed loving, gentle and kind in the beginning. That's why I was so taken aback the first time he called me a bitch. I automatically took responsibility, for doing something to push him over the edge. I immediately came up with an excuse to justify his anger, which allowed me to accept his apology. It was like a game of Russian roulette, which he would win. I gave into my fear of being alone and what I thought was my love for him.

It was late at night and we were outside arguing. I wasn't walking at the speed he liked and some random guys started whistling at me. He was mad and accused me of never listening and called me a stupid bitch. He then hit me so hard in my abdomen that I collapsed to the floor. I couldn't breathe. The blow was so debilitating. Sometimes, I still feel the pain sporadically. As I was lying on the cold ground, holding my stomach, crying, an overwhelming fear came over me. I thought this could be the last night of my young life. Somehow, I found the courage to get up and run for my life. That's when these three strangers came to my aid. When they offered assistance, I assured them that I was okay. When he walked up on us with his friends, the strangers seemed to know that there was more going on. They looked at me with kindness and concern in their eyes and one of them said, "Come with us". In that moment I knew the choice I had to make. I knew that if I chose to go with him, that would be the end of me. At that moment, I knew I had to choose me. And just like that, I was done. I drove off with three complete strangers. Can you imagine the danger I must have felt to get in a car with three people that I had never met? Can you imagine being in complete fear of and abused and manipulated by the person you love? The love I thought I had was tainted with abuse, control, manipulation, and fear. Real love had become a foreign concept to me. I didn't understand what love was supposed to be or how it was supposed to feel. I just knew that I wanted and needed to be loved. Most importantly, I didn't know how to love and care for myself.

From my childhood until well into my adult life I had so many experiences that skewed my perception of love. Although I had amazing parents and a family who truly loved me, I still had many misconceptions of love. We all have our own issues, pains, struggles, and challenges. I had

gotten so used to anger, abuse, and unhealthy relationships.

I never had an example of real, true, healthy, reciprocated

love. Chaos and dysfunction was my normal, which had

made my current view of relationships skewed, thinking

that this was just the way relationships were. Even with all

of the dysfunction and rollercoaster moments in my own

relationship, I believed that he loved me and that I loved

him. I understood that he had so many issues that he never

dealt and I was willing to look past every one of them,

sacrificing myself for him. I was sympathetic to his

behavior and enabled it because I didn't feel like I deserved

anything more than what he was currently giving me. There

were some good times and I held onto those moments so

that I could cope with the verbal, mental, and emotional

abuse. Our relationship was unhealthy and toxic. There is

always a breaking point, when you become fed up, and

something has to give. This is my story. This was my breaking point.

I was working three jobs at once, trying to support myself and my boyfriend. I felt a little uneasy as I went to bed, he was acting a little weird. I was a little fearful and on edge but tried to sleep, quietly so I didn't disturb him. I woke up bright and early in the morning. My worries from the night before slipped away as I rested. It was a new day and I was excited, it was my first day off in months.

I had barely wiped the drool off of my face when my amazing morning turned into a complete nightmare in a split second. My boyfriend appeared, not with breakfast in bed, but a look of wrath and rage. In that moment, I was overwhelmed with fear, my palms started to sweat, and my hands started to shake. In a slight panic, I began to wonder what could I have done or said, and reluctantly I asked, "What's wrong?" "You remember a few weeks ago, you told me you went on a date while we were on a break?" he said. I immediately flashed back to the conversation he was talking about.

We have had a tumultuous relationship for years. I finally felt I had the courage enough to end our relationship. For a couple of months, I was victorious and cut all contact with him but he did not stop harassing me. I had a temporary order of protection against him but the police couldn't or at least wouldn't help me. Eventually, I just gave in and we started talking again. He slithered his way back in like he had done some many other times in the past. He allowed me to be comfortable and to begin to think he had really changed this time. He had promised he had changed so many times and I wanted to believe him. One random day, he admitted that he was seeing other people and had been with other women. He asked, "Did you sleep with or date any other men while we were on a break?" I have always tried to be honest, I responded, "Yes, one date." "Did you kiss him? Did you sleep with him? Do you talk to him still?" he asked. "No, I did none of those things and I never spoke to or saw him again after the date." I replied. I was so nervous and scared during the entire date. I didn't have the opportunity to enjoy it. I was scared that my then ex would walk in on us or nervous that one of his friends could see me. Even though I cut off contact with him he still had control over my life.

"Yes," I replied, "I remember when I told you I went on a date." "Did you like the dude? You must have to be on a date with him." He said. I instantly got up and started getting dressed. Although I was terrified, I couldn't show it. I couldn't let him see the fear I was feeling because me becoming afraid seemed to empower him in an evil way. "I am not doing this with you this morning, this is my first day off in forever." I said, "I don't understand why you can't let it go. I am not going to stay here if this is how the day is going to be." I start walking out the room past him with my stuff. In that moment, I felt like I was paralyzed with fear of what he might do. He followed behind me cursing and yelling. "So, you don't care? You stupid bitch!" he yelled. I was out the door and in the elevator at this time. He held the door open with his foot. I felt like Satan himself was staring back at me. "You don't care?" he yelled. "No" I replied. I was tired and couldn't believe that I was back here. What was I doing? How did I get back to this place? My entire life flashed before my eyes. He punched me. He punched me in the face. I felt so helpless and I was scared for my life. He punched me again and another time. He hit me so hard that my head hit the back elevator wall. My headscarf flew off and I fell onto the floor. My head throbbing, my face was on fire and I couldn't tell where the pain was coming from or what damage he could have done. At this point, the elevator door starts to close. He leaves me. Alone. Laying on the floor of an elevator, bleeding, crying. I start to gather my things off of the floor. My mind was racing. I felt like I was going to die and that I would never make it out of this building. He had never hit me like that before. I was filled with fear. I was scared that once the elevator door opened he would be there ready to finish me and I would be no more. The door opened and to my relief he wasn't there. I bolted towards the door, at the same time I felt something starting to drip from my mouth. Instinctively, placed my hand up to catch whatever it could be. I looked down, blood was pouring from my mouth. In a panic I burst outside to look for a cab as the blood was pooling in my hand. I didn't know what to do. "COME BACK INSIDE!" It was the voice I knew all too well. The devil reincarnated. "You are causing a scene, come back inside!" he said. I could barely open my mouth, my hand was full of blood, and I felt pain in my entire body. He ran across the street and came back with paper towel. Luckily in the instant, I saw a cab and I bolted towards it. He tried to stop me but I had to save my life. I had to finally choose me.

Finally, after what seemed like the longest cab ride ever I reached my house, rushed to the bathroom to access the damage. I looked in the mirror in complete shock. My mouth was busted open and the entire right side of my face was swollen to the point that I was unrecognizable. Tears just streamed down my face and mixed with my blood. As I began to clean myself up I knew that in this moment I had had enough. This was my moment. I choose me. I reconnected with the person I once was filled with hope, and dreams of a better life. I remembered her. I allowed that hope to begin to live again.

Relationships are supposed to uplift your spirit and build you up. I was so beaten down physically, mentally, emotionally, and spiritually by my relationship that I felt broken, weak, depressed, and even suicidal. I finally found the courage to leave. I had to find a way to forgive the man that inflicted so much pain on my body and in my emotions. I had to find a way to navigate through all the hurt and pain and forgive him even without the apology that I knew I would never hear. Allowing this man to continue to rob me of my joy, to dim my light, and control my life was no longer an option. I had to find a way to let go of the hurt and the pain so that I could be free. I had to forgive him I didn't have a choice. I had to let go of fear and be courageous enough to take my power back. In the beginning I had to fake it but I refused to let this man make me feel powerless, inferior, depressed, or to take my life. Sometimes you have to fake it before you make it. I also had to forgive myself for continually putting myself into an unsafe situation. I had to forgive myself for not valuing my own life. I am sometimes my own worst enemy. I am so hard on myself. I felt I should have known better, I was embarrassed and I felt so weak and damaged. I had to work through all of the emotions and the trauma. I had been mentally, emotionally, and physically abused for years. I found a therapist to guide me through my journey of inner healing. I took it a step further and found an amazing life coach. The key was not allowing my past to define my future.

Sometimes the choice has to be made; either you or them. When enough is enough. When your happiness enough. Your love is enough. Your joy is enough. I made that choice. I knew that enough was enough. I deserved to be cherished and loved. First, I had to learn to love myself unconditionally and to never settle for anything less than I deserve. The first part of the journey was learning how to love myself, what I wanted, what deserve, and self-value. I had to constantly remind myself that I am enough. If I never made the decision to love myself I may not be here today. I am grateful for all of my trials and tribulations because it has made me into the beautiful woman I am today. It has allowed me to understand maximizing continually in order to evolve instantly. In order for us to have maximum evolution we must overcome adversities.

In life, we will experience adversities and trauma through relationship and heartbreak, we need to understand our past or current circumstances do not define who we are or who we will become unless we allow it to. I am enough. You are enough.

Journey to Happily Ever After

LaQuista Erinna

War changes people. After completing two deployments to
Iraq, I can definitely say that I am not the same person that
I used to be. Love makes things even more complicated. I
was only 22 years old when I first deployed. I was young,
scared, and had no real responsibilities. Never in a million
years did I imagine I would deploy again, and to go to the
same war was unimaginable. Things were different the
second time around. I had a new husband and a son.
Although things weren't perfect, we were making it work. I
remember when I first got my orders. I cried in bed to my
first husband and made him promise me that if I didn't
make it back alive, he would raise our son near my family.
I wanted Jordan to know my family and remember me as
his mother. I spent a year in Iraq and it was very difficult to
readjust to being a wife, a mother; just being myself. Post-
traumatic stress disorder (PTSD) caused a strain on our
relationship. My first husband had his own set of issues

which were only magnified by my problems. I didn't recognize him as my best friend anymore. Instead, he was a stranger and we felt more like roommates than anything else. He began to drink more and more, but never would admit he had a problem. Things got so bad where I was afraid of who would come home, Dr. Jekyll or Mr. Hyde. That's when I knew it was time to leave. Jordan was only five years old, but asked me, "Mom, why don't you find someone who loves you?" This broke my heart but also confirmed that it was time to move on. Children, no matter how young, are watching. I realized that I was raising a young, black boy, who would someday be someone's significant other. It's my responsivity to show him positive examples of relationships and love.

Dating after divorce was not only hard, but nearly impossible. After being married, you tend to forget all the nuances of dating. Dating in the Atlanta is an entirely different animal. I tried everything from online dating to blind dates to saying "yes" to guys that I would never consider dating under normal circumstances. I usually don't get approached by too many men when I go out. I'm 5'11" and have a pretty strong 'resting bitch face.' It takes a particularly confidant man to even approach me, and to be honest, I'm usually focused on some personal mini crisis to even notice if a guy is checking me out. One day while getting my car serviced at the dealership, a stranger struck up a conversation with me. In between playing on my phone and half listening, I almost didn't notice how handsome he was. After my car was finished, and I paid, the guy asked if he could have my phone number. I was happy to hear from him a couple days later and we made plans to go out for dinner. If you don't already know the rules of dating, you never let a guy pick you up from your house. There are a lot of weird people in the world, and why invite unnecessary drama into your life when you haven't even decided if you like this person. We met in a neutral location for an early dinner. Things were going fairly well until we had both finished our meal and had to actually talk. He proceeded to tell me how he wasn't looking for a woman who already had her own. "Excuse me?" He stated that he preferred to date women who didn't already own a home, who didn't drive a luxury car, who didn't have too much education. "Too much education?" I asked him to clarify because I couldn't possibly be hearing what I thought I just heard. He explained that he would much rather have a woman that didn't have these things so they could build something together. At that point, I knew I would never have talked to this guy again. I nervously laughed and told him that I didn't think we would make it to a second date. After making it home, I thought more about the ridiculous date I just had. I was offended. Why is it that men punish a woman for being successful? At that point in my life, I wasn't where I wanted to be, but I had accomplished some bit of success. I owned my own home and had two cars. I had a good job. Although I didn't make a lot of money, there was enough to take care of my son and all our needs. I had two bachelor's degrees, but most importantly, I didn't depend on a man to take care of me. Men are always saying they don't want to take care of a woman, but some are intimidated by a woman who isn't dependent upon them.

In 2013, I received a promotion that required me to move to Minnesota. Everyone was shocked that I actually accepted the position but for me it was a no brainer. After my divorce, I struggled to find a meaningful relationship. Being a thirty-something year old woman, society tells you that you must have a man to have it all. After you've been single for a period of time, you get used to doing it all on your own. It can be challenging to consider a man's opinion when you're used to calling all the shots. I viewed the move to Minnesota as a stepping stone to further my career. After all my failed relationships, I knew I had to really focus on my career so that I could provide the best life for my son. I was only in Minnesota for about a year before accepting a position in my career field as a Social Worker. Without hesitation, I packed my things and headed on to a new adventure in Connecticut. I rented a beautiful townhome in the quiet town of Ellington. It reminded me of my hometown and gave me a sense of peace. One day while grabbing lunch at Panera Bread, I had a very casual conversation with the only other black person in line. He commented that I looked like I worked out and stated that he was a personal trainer. While thinking to myself, "yeah, right" I decided to give him my number. It was nearly a month later before I returned his phone calls. More than anything, I wanted to get back in shape. I require constant motivation to stay consistent with working out. He began training me and eventually we started dating. I quickly fell head over heels for him.

Unfortunately, he was more into work than me. It didn't end badly, but I was still devastated about having another failed relationship. I was away from home, just me and my son. I reached out to the only other local friend I had. Erick was a charismatic guy and so easy to talk to. We met at my new Army Reserve unit, and I began tutoring him. He wanted to go from enlisted to officer and needed to retake his ASVAB test. We built up a decent friendship after hours of tutoring on Skype and a few in person sessions. He lived in Boston, about two hours from me, so it wasn't easy to meet on a regular basis. He was there to comfort me during my breakup. I was surprised when he sent an Edible Arrangement to my job the following week. I invited him over to watch a movie and was surprised that he actually made the drive to my place. We stayed up for hours just talking. It was at this point that I realized how much we had in common. We eventually started dating and things progressed extremely fast. As corny as it may sound, we talked about marriage and children. He was the most

thoughtful man I had ever been with. Every need that I had,

he fulfilled even before I knew it was a need of mine's. We

began planning a life together and decided to move in with

one another.

A couple of months into our romance, I found out I was

pregnant. I was excited but nervous to tell him. I think

when I told him, he was terrified. His initial reaction was

excitement but I could hear the fear and uncertainty in his

voice. He wasn't ready. Before finding out that I was

pregnant, I told him that I wanted one more child but only

if I got pregnant before the age of 35. I felt like I could not

have any more children and was being punished by God. A

few years prior, I was pregnant by an ex and pressured to

have an abortion. I swore that I would never let another

person pressure me into doing anything that I didn't want to

do. He promised me that we would be able to have children

together. He said that although I was a few years older than him, he believed that it would take no time for us to conceive. He was right, because before we could even move in together, I was staring at a positive pregnancy test. Imagine my surprise when a couple of days later, he tells me that things are moving too fast and he's not ready to move in with me. To be clear, we weren't breaking up; he just was not ready to move in together. If that wasn't a clear sign, I don't know what else it could have been. We still tried to make our relationship work, but things went downhill fast. Because of my age, I was considered high risk. Who knew that a 35-year-old woman was approaching *advanced maternal age*? The baby was due one day after my thirty fifth birthday so technically, I would be 36, making me high risk. I had a lot of appointments with specialists to make sure everything was okay. I felt alone and decided I needed to be home with family when I was about six months along. I told him that I was moving back to Georgia and I hoped he would come with me. He promised that he would ask to be transferred to Georgia but he had to wait until his active duty orders were up. He never went to any of my doctor's appointments. He never seemed to care how me and the baby were doing. My mother had been living in my house since I moved to Minnesota. I rented a four-bedroom house in hopes that Erick and his daughter would join us. That never happened and I knew it was over. I was terribly depressed. Throughout my pregnancy, I gained over 60 pounds. At 10 years old, Jordan was my biggest helper. Surprisingly, my ex-husband, was also there for me. He would come by the house and help out and make sure me and the baby were okay. I know it hurt him when he found out I was pregnant. I was embarrassed and felt like the biggest failure. Here I am, 35 years old, unmarried, alone, and pregnant. Raising two boys on my own scared the crap out of me. I didn't know how I was going to do it. Thankfully I was able to transfer from my job in Connecticut to Atlanta. Although I didn't receive a warm welcome on my first day, I had security knowing I couldn't be fired. I remember my first official day at the Atlanta VA. I never told them I was pregnant. I know, I know, they can't discriminate against me due to my pregnancy, but we all know they find other ways to not give you the job. The Program Chief made a snarky remark. My supervisor took me around to introduce me and my pregnant belly to all the staff. The Chief took one look at my belly and said, "How long do we have you before you're out? Let me stop before I get an EO complaint." She then walked off. She seemed annoyed that I was just started and would be going out on maternity leave soon. Every day that I went into that office was pure hell. Physically, it was a strain on my body but the hostile environment was just too much. I begged my doctor to take me out of maternity leave. I eventually got my wish at the beginning on November. With no short-term disability, I knew that it was going to be rough. There was not much communication with Erick. I started to hate him. He was out living his life and I was struggling to keep my head above water. My mother told me I looked pitiful and she couldn't wait for me to have the baby.

My water broke the day after Thanksgiving. My mom came over to take me to the hospital. I hesitated but I called to tell Erick that I was in labor. He told me he was on his way to training in Kentucky and would call to check on me. Jackson was born on November 28, 2015. I stayed in the hospital for a couple days before we were released. It felt weird having a new baby after all these years. I was sleep deprived and had a terrible headache. I asked my mother to watch the baby while I went to urgent care. I didn't feel right and wanted to make sure I wasn't having a reaction to the epidural. That ER visit turned into me being admitted to the hospital. My blood pressure was so high; the doctor was surprised I didn't have a stroke. I was strapped to my hospital bed so I wouldn't have to get up. I freaked out! It was just too much for one person to handle. Thankfully my family was able to watch the kids while I was in the hospital.

Going through all of this, my hatred for Erick grew even more. He should be here with me; supporting me. Slowly I began to feel like myself again. I returned back to work and applied for an active duty tour. Erick and I would talk occasionally but he hadn't changed. He asked me to move to Boston so he could be in our son's life. I refused. He wanted everything on his terms and I couldn't move and leave my support system. Not after he had betrayed and hurt me so badly. As time went on, I slowly started to forget about him. He wasn't the only man in the world. He went on with his life and I so did I. I didn't get into any serious relationships after him. I accepted that I might be single for a while and I was okay with that. When Jackson was about a year and a half, I reached out to Erick via email. I couldn't understand why he didn't want to be in our son's life. He replied back and his response infuriated me. He told me that he had a girlfriend and to please let him go. Let him go? I just wanted him to be in Jackson's life. My fingers were typing so fast; I don't even remember what my response was but it certainly wasn't nice. I asked my good friend, to read the emails and let me know if I was overreacting. She has a way of being brutally honest, but it is all out of love. When she read all our email responses, she told me that she felt he was scared. She thought we just needed a mediator and to come up with a plan for co-parenting. I agreed and assured her he wouldn't participate. To my surprise we were finally able to speak on the phone without arguing. I listened to him and he listened to me. He asked if he could fly me and Jackson to Boston so he could spend some time with him. I agreed. I didn't know what to expect seeing him after all this time. He met us at the gate, and I got butterflies. I felt like I wanted to throw up. I handed Jackson to him and walked hurriedly to baggage claim. For the next few days, it felt good to watch him care for our son. It was like he had never missed a beat.

After we flew back home, communication with Erick improved. I respected his relationship but felt that I had to tell him that I still had feelings for him. I didn't know these feelings still existed until I saw him. I think I scared him at first. It was days later that he told me he always wanted us but felt that he had messed up so badly and I would never take him back. He said he needed time to end his relationship and asked me to be patient. I agreed but didn't really expect much. The same man that refused to bend was now making plans. He knew exactly what I expected. He left his job and came to North Carolina to be with us. I was planning to come off of active duty and we would be moving back to Georgia. We begin couples counseling and had some major breakthroughs. He managed to get active duty orders for Atlanta. Erick stayed with my cousin and made the four-hour drive to North Carolina every weekend.

We were all set to be a real family. Unexpectedly he got active duty orders to go to New Jersey. He wanted me to join him. I refused to pick up my life and move without a real commitment. There was still some pain there. Erick refused to go without me and asked me to marry him. I couldn't believe this was happening. I agreed. We had two weeks to plan our courthouse nuptials.

July 27, 2017, I married the man that was made for me. We said our vows in front of a few special loved ones. Throughout my journey I learned some important things about myself. I learned that I never thought I deserved to be truly happy because of my own insecurities. In school, I was always picked on for being too skinny or too tall or not cute enough. I was told I had a big nose and a flat chest. I also grew up seeing women in my family accept less than they deserved from men. In turn, I accepted the same. As a black woman you have to be nothing less than excellent. This time around, I refused to comprise my standards. Once

I knew my own worth, it was unacceptable to entertain anything less than. When a man is ready and he wants to truly be with you, he will move heaven and Earth to make it happen. Erick and I share so much and he supports me in everything I do. I have never been happier in my life. Today I am living my truth and it GLOWS all over me. I am living MY happily ever after.

To Be Young and Free

Andrea M. Stuckey

"The old believe everything, the middle-aged suspect everything,
the young know everything."

-Oscar Wilde

Oh, to be young and free. That is how I was feeling at the

age of 22. I had been in the military, finished up my

radiology certification and was stationed at the United

States Military Academy in West Point, New York. I was

finally feeling accomplished. Upon my arrival at West

Point, unbeknown to me, I met my first husband whom we

will call Wayne. On the day of my arrival, Wayne was the

soldier on duty who was responsible for checking me in

and showing me to my living quarters. There was an

immediate attraction upon our introduction, and we found

ourselves eventually spending time together and dating.

After only five months of dating, Wayne proposed to me

and shortly thereafter, we found ourselves having a very

small sweet chapel wedding as many young soldiers in the

military decide to do. Oh yes, to be young and in love, we did everything together. We went to the movies, we entertained with friends and we even grocery shopped together. What a fun season of life. It was simply so easy to be. We explored all the sites of New York City and traveled throughout New England. I was living a wonderful life with my best friend.

What I learned early on with Wayne, was that he had a very charismatic and attractive personality, along with being very handsome. Whenever he walked into a room, people were immediately drawn to him. However, with all, one of the factors that I chose to ignore early in the relationship was that with his charismatic personality was an underlying flirtatiousness that Wayne had with women. I convinced myself that because of the nature of the military and the constant ways that women and men had to interact, that they were just platonic friendships among Wayne and a lot of women. However, I would come to find out in several years that this underlying flirtatiousness would become a greater problem.

Shortly after our marriage, my military contract ended, and I became a military wife. I found a fantastic job at a local urgent care center and began working. Within a year, Wayne received orders to be deployed overseas to Egypt and the Gaza Strip area. We would soon find ourselves separated for an extended time. Prior to that deployment we chose to move away from New York to be closer to another Army base that he desired to be stationed at upon his return from overseas. We packed up all our belongings and to another state prior to his actual deployment overseas. We were not looking forward to the initial military separation of six months. It was difficult for us to imagine because we really had been the very best of friends doing everything together. However, we decided that we would make it work. We moved to a state where I had previously lived prior to entering the Army. While Wayne was away, I decided that I would work, visit old friends, find a new church, make new friends and keep myself as busy as possible. During the separation, we managed our relationship through calls and traditional mail at that time. The first six months went by quickly and Wayne was finally able to come home for about 30 days or so. We quickly picked up where we left off. Visiting family and friends and traveling as well. Shortly thereafter, Wayne returned to his overseas duty station for another six months. Upon his return to the States, he received a new duty station about eight hours away from where we lived. He was home for several months before reporting there. During that time, we reconnected, joined a church that we loved, traveled and went to visit family and friends. I soon became pregnant and we were both extremely excited. We decided that we would continue our long distance marriage until the baby was born. After the birth, we would all move together to his duty station in Georgia. We kept the marriage fun for the first few months. I'd drive down to Georgia for some weekends and some weekends he'd drive home. We would have a wonderful time anticipating, planning, and discussing the birth of our first-born child. When I became about 6 months or so, I could feel the shift in our relationship. The pattern of our calls and his visits home changed. He made excuses about the nature of the changes, but I felt that there was something going on that I couldn't put my hands on.

During the holiday week of Thanksgiving, we planned that he would come home, and we would have dinner and visit with family and friends. I was super excited, proudly pregnant and feeling the holiday vibes. He was to come home on that Wednesday before Thanksgiving. He called that morning saying that he had a car accident and that he was alright, but he had to take care of all the matters concerning it and that he would just catch a train home the following morning. I was just glad that he was alright and not hurt. I woke up on Thanksgiving morning and I began cooking the traditional Thanksgiving dinner. I felt proud of my little belly, and excited that my husband would be home for the holiday. As the time for his train to arrive approached, I quickly changed my clothes, put on a cute maternity outfit, refreshed my make-up and hair, and went to the train station to pick him up. His trained arrived, and I looked for him with great anticipation and excitement. I looked at every person getting off the train because it was a small train station. He was not a passenger on the train. He did not get off. The train began to pull off and my heart sank. Why wouldn't he call if he missed the train or was travelling in another way.? I was extremely disappointed. I got in my car and cried all the way back to the house. When I got home, I called the army barracks and did not get an answer. Everyone was gone, it was Thanksgiving. Where was he?

I cried and cried, too embarrassed to visit anyone because I didn't know what to say about Wayne's whereabouts. I ate a little food and spent most of the next two days in bed, still calling the barracks, not getting any answer nor receiving any contact from Wayne. This was way before the cell phone era. There was no way to contact him. At one point I called the State troopers of VA, NC, and Georgia to see if he was in an accident. He wasn't. He finally appeared Saturday morning as if all was fine and dandy. I hit the roof! He had lame excuses regarding the accident and missing the train and saying that he knew I would be mad so that's why he didn't call. I did not accept his excuses and the distance and tension in our relationship became evident. Who would leave their pregnant wife alone on a holiday and not communicate with her? A man who was seeing another woman.

That weekend, I was looking for keys in his coat and found a letter from a young woman professing her love for him and that she'd wait for our baby to be born and the divorce if she had to. My stomach dropped. Wayne was seeing a young woman who was one of his soldiers. I angrily took the letter and confronted him about it. He was calm and acted as if it was a young girl with a crush on him. He denied all my allegations. I knew better, but was scared stiff. Here I was pregnant with my first child, away from my biological family, and my church family thought that he was the greatest guy ever. What would I do? I acted as if I believed him, but I knew deep down he was having an affair. I then felt out of shape and envious with my pregnant belly. I began to internalize this stress which caused me to go into pre-term labor about two months later. I was in and out of the hospital trying to prevent my daughter from being born too early. Wayne was aloof and there were more missed calls, absent days, and no show visits. He managed to get time off from the Army during my last month of pregnancy to attend pregnancy classes and be available for the birth of our daughter. We interacted as normally as possible, but I felt that something was still off.

I gave birth to our beautiful daughter, Victoria. We both basked in parenthood and the beauty of our daughter. We were excited to show her to the world, family and friends. Victoria was almost two weeks old and I received a call that my father had passed away. I was crushed. The plethora of hormone changes that I was already experiencing heightened as I had to prepare to go to my home state of Connecticut to bury my father with a two-week old in tow. I was devastated.

As life plays out and specific cards are dealt to us, God gives us an immeasurable amount of grace to endure. Grace that is needed before major challenges arise. After returning from the unspeakable event of burying my father and all the family emotional drama that goes along with it, I returned home with my husband and new daughter to prepare to move our home to Georgia. We would now take on a new life, in a new place with a fresh start, so I thought. It took a few days to get the moving van all packed up with the help of friends. We finally got on the road and my friend Janet and her husband drove to Georgia with us to help with our transition since she had a sister in that area. We arrived safely in Georgia and were able to find temporary housing with the military as we waited for the availability of permanent housing. It took a few days to get settled into our temporary space, and I was beginning to feel a little relief, as I was physically and emotionally exhausted. One afternoon, I had just put Victoria down for a nap and Wayne was watching television in the bedroom and the telephone rang. It was a call from the receptionist in the lobby of where we were staying. She informed me that a young woman was there to visit us. In a split second, my mind and my spirit already knew who this was and what this visit was about. I wanted details, so I said, "Send her up!"

Two minutes later there was a light knock at the door and I opened the door. Standing there was a young woman about nineteen years old, wearing a white maternity blouse and a skirt. I had never seen her before. I didn't even flinch. I stared at her. She didn't know what to think. I motioned for her to come in. The power of God took over my body and I was in complete control. I shut the door and said firmly "What do you want? I already know." She was speechless because of my calmness. She didn't receive the reaction that she was looking for. She began to cry and get upset saying "He told me you guys were getting a divorce!" As her voice elevated, and I stood there unmoved, Wayne heard the commotion and came out of the bedroom. When he saw her, he freaked out and started yelling at her. "What are you doing here?" She was crying and saying somethings that I don't even remember. They were going back and forth as I stood unmoved, shocked but calm. I finally said, "Stop it!" I looked at the young woman and stared at her and said "I feel sorry for you, that you've gotten yourself caught up in this mess. You can leave now." I opened the door, never acknowledging her 5-month pregnant belly, and motioned for her to leave. I shut the door behind her, stared at it, as I felt like my whole entire body was about to explode into pieces. I turned around, looked at Wayne, and lost it. "How could you be so stupid to cheat on me AND not use protection and get another woman pregnant!!" I began screaming and yelling as he began to attempt to defend himself. He eventually left, and I laid down and cried my heart out. What was I going to do? I just had a newborn, lost my father, quit a very good job to move to support my husband, and that was what I walked into. I was devastated.

After a couple of days of crying, and arguing with Wayne back and forth, I finally asked him what he really wanted.

If he wanted to stay with HER, or his family. He pleaded that he was sorry and that he wanted our family. I chose to forgive him, and we did go to a few sessions of military marital counseling. The next step was to reconcile the child issues with the other woman etc. She decided to leave the Army and go back home to Detroit to have her baby. I was adamant about Wayne supporting his responsibility as a father, and he drew up a contract of what child support would look like. We discussed commitment boundaries and how I was to be aware of all communication and plans in regards of the baby. I can't even express what a tough time this was in my life. I was embarrassed and ashamed, and I told absolutely no one in my family. I carried the load all alone and had a ton of migraines to go with it. I wanted to try to make my marriage work. I had a beautiful young daughter whom Wayne absolutely adored, and I didn't want to take that away from her. My faith and being a member of a small intimate church where we lived, was an integral part of keeping my mind together. God gives us the strength that we need, when we need it most.

After a few months, things were flowing somewhat normally from day to day. I was still bearing a heavy load because I knew that the other woman's child would be born soon. Wayne received the call of the birth of their son – Ishmael. The young woman was the daughter of a pastor, and really took the birth of her son as a literal expression of a biblical context. My heart sank more. I found a part-time job where I worked 4:00pm-7pm. It was perfect. I could be with Victoria during the day, and when Wayne came home at 3pm I could head out to work before 4pm. It gave me a much needed out, and sense of purpose. I began to feel better about myself.

About a year later, Wayne was due to re-enlist in the Army, however the fact that Wayne was the leader of the young woman who became pregnant, the Army suggested that he not re-enlist versus undergoing charges of fraternization.

Our military family career was over. We had to move and return to civilian life. We decided to move back to Virginia where we had a beautiful church family and friends to support us and our young marriage.

We returned to Virginia and stayed with Victoria's Godparents for about two months until Wayne found a job and we found a new apartment. Victoria was a little over a year old and things were going relatively smoothly. I was excited again about a new beginning and having more supportive friends around. There was still a lot of marital tension and stress from the changes but that was to be expected, so I thought. After living in our new apartment for about a month, we received our first telephone bill. There weren't cell phones back then, so every long-distance call was listed on the bill. As I reviewed the phone bill, there it was, tons of calls to the young woman. Calls that were hours at a time, without any of my knowledge. I felt ultimately betrayed. I was done. I had sacrificed so much and been hurt to my core and he was still being deceptive. I decided to confront him. When he arrived home that evening, I showed him the bill and gave him an ultimatum. The ultimatum was for us to go to marital counseling at our church which would require accountability, or he would have to leave. He stated that he was not going to counseling. I said, "Then you've got to go!"

The next day, I had just started a new part-time job at a hospital, and I was undergoing training. Wayne was off and stayed with Victoria during the day. I came home that afternoon and saw his duffel bag in the hall. Victoria was napping. We had not spoken since the conversation the night before. I went into the bedroom to change my clothes and I heard him call a cab. I laid on the bed and part of me was nervous and part of me was thinking "Just let him leave." I had been through so much deception; I was mentally exhausted. I heard him go into Victoria's room, then I heard the cab honk the horn. Just like that, he grabbed his duffel bag, walked out without a good bye, and I have never seen him again. As of this writing, Victoria is 24 years old.

Initially, I felt relieved but as the weeks passed and there was no type of correspondence, I realized the truth of the matter. The marriage was over. Being abandoned with a toddler, was extremely overwhelming. I am grateful that my family who were 8 hours away, came to help me with my daughter in shifts of weeks at a time until I could solidify childcare and transportation. I literally had to rebuild my life with a toddler in tow. There were times where I really thought that I was going to have a nervous breakdown, and there were times where I was counting change at the grocery store to make sure Victoria and I could eat until payday.

I continued to go to church on a regular basis and build my faith and relationship with God. Every time that I had a need, God sent a person or a way to provide that need. As a believer, I understand the importance of faith and work to go with that faith. Resting on our laurels will not grant us provision. However, when we couple up with God through Jesus Christ in relationship, there is nothing that is too great for us to handle and overcome. As a young single Mom, I built my skill set in my career, and continued to build my faith. I surrounded myself with supportive people, places and things and God literally opened doors that I know only He could do.

It almost seems surreal that I endured these life challenges in my mid-twenties, but I learned the importance of patience, identifying counterfeits, trusting my spirit, how strong I really am with God on my side, and I learned that relationships are complex and require real work and commitment. You might walk through the fire, but you will not be burned. Tough situations build a stronger faith. A faith that you can use not only for yourself, but for others

who come across your path along life's journey.

I Know What It Means to Love Me
Rashida Ingram

I remember the initial feelings of terror and joy upon
finding out that I was pregnant. Who would have thought
that I would be pregnant at 21 years old? What was the
purpose? What was I destined to do? Who am I? For a brief
moment, I remember trying to make it all makes sense
however there was no time. A baby was coming right? I felt
nervous, happy and excited all at the same time. Mike and I
had only known each other for a short time. We were
friends, but could we co-parent? I really did not know.
Time was moving forward. I was in my last year of
undergrad working the 3pm-11pm. Every part of me said to
embrace life as it comes. Mike was an excellent man and
thirteen years my senior. I was just beginning to live my
life. I was comfortable with my daily routine. I was a
college student, living independently in an off campus
apartment. I was taking care of myself. Unfortunately, my
initiation into womanhood would involve heartache. That's

what happens when you don't have a set of criteria for what you are looking for in a mate.

In the mind of this 20-year-old, I believed that if I was nice and treated people with love and kindness, they would love me back. I learned that I was wrong in that assumption. My open-heart was a love magnet to those who knew that they wanted love, but they were unable to reciprocate. My inhibition was down and my self-worth was sinking even lower. To keep my mind afloat, I continued my routine of working, going to school, maintaining my household and visiting with friends and family. On the surface things appeared stable. For the most part life was a structured routine. From an outside view I appeared to have everything in tack. Mike started to give me a ride home from work during the nights that we both got off at 11pm. We would talk about work, life and of course relationships. The more I talked the more Mike seemed to fit the profile of a perfect gentleman. He would open my car door, censor his language, act as if he wasn't a chain smoker, and he made no issue about his act of chivalry. At times, I felt the disconnection but forged ahead away. Why not, after all we were treating each other well.

As time passed and I settled into my relationship with Mike I became comfortable in my adjustment to life as his girlfriend. Soon after we decided to make it official we found out that I was pregnant. We initially were shocked. I did not know what to think. As the news traveled throughout our job others were thrilled. Mike and Rashida couldn't be any more deserving of a baby together. We always heard how we were such good people and all. So, I settled in a little more into the relationship, yet I still required the freedom to explore life and to go through my own process of self-discovery. At that moment of transition along with the news of a baby coming very soon I sprang into action. I certainly knew that I was responsible, mature and capable of doing my best. I wanted to become excited about life and about the fact that I was preparing to raise another human being. However, my intuition was saying something different. Mike's perfect image was unraveling. What I wanted and needed in my life began to take precedent over just being satisfied with having a man. Once Mike and I lived together full time our mask came down more and more. Mike began to take the keys so that I could not get to work. He also attempted to monitor how much money I had in my wallet from day to day. Despite the signs of control, I forged ahead, thinking what do I have to lose? However, the question should have been what I am gaining emotionally and how am I thriving psychologically. The truth of the matter is that I really was not gaining anything from the relationship; and I did not have anything left to give.

Mike became obsesses with how we looked together. Yet on the inside I was miserable and depressed. I had fallen into a pattern of trying to keep the peace while he wanted to take control of the simplest detail. Even with all of that, I was home one Sunday morning and I read the headline in the newspaper "MILLENNIUM WEDDING 2000!!" I said to Mike as he sat at the other end of the couch, "we should do this, who else would put up with us; we might as well get married." It was expected. We felt it and had been told several times by our friends, coworkers and family. A simple greeting went from hello to "so when are you two getting married." Without a second thought or a critical examination of our love for each other, Mike said "You're right we should just get married." And that was it, we decided to get married. Not because we loved each other, I married Mike because I was not prepared to do anything else.

I entered into a marriage without a sense of identity. When I think about my years as a child and the relationships that I was exposed to; I did not have close contact with anyone who was in a healthy relationship. My mother was never married, my father was absent from my life and my grandparents divorced very early in my childhood. Furthermore, I also spent more time with single women, than I did with folks in relationships. I did not have a concrete clue about what a successful relationship looked like. I damn sure did not know how to create one. Therefore, I normalized dysfunction. One day I did not tell Mike that I had $10 left over from paying the cable bill. Mike became so upset that he pushed me against the wall. Thank God that his mother was visiting that day. She came rushing up the stairs breathing heavily through her tracheotomy. "MIKE get your hands off of her right now!" He did so immediately. I grabbed my daughter and left the house for a few hours. Once he calmed down he apologized, and his mother also called to inform me that she told him that he better not ever put his hands on me again. In my mind I knew there was nothing she could do. If Mike could not control everything about me he quickly lost all emotional control. Which meant that I was being pushed or grabbed on for some reason or another. While staring at my reflection, I thought about my mother crying, after being pushed around by my father. That's when I noticed my daughter staring at me. I wondered what she thought of me.

I received a job as a Family Based Therapist immediately after graduation. There, I worked with a woman who was severely beaten by her husband and left wheelchair bound. I was starting to detach from Mike. My soul was deteriorating, and I felt like I was living a lie. How can I counsel anyone with the life I'm living? Mike was becoming more and more jealous with each step that I made towards living as a young woman. We did not speak the same language, and there was no understanding of who each other was becoming. One night after yet another terrible argument, I packed up Miya and went to a crap hole motel. Mike was constantly badgering me this particular night about a recommendation letter that I asked one of the psychologists at our job to write for me. He could not understand why I had to email him information about myself in order for him to draft the recommendation letter. I was exhausted. Yet he would not let up. When he went to work the next day I took a cab to the Days Inn. As my daughter and I slept I heard a knock at the door. "Rashida, Rashida, let me in!" I opened the door and there he stood. "Rashida don't leave me like this, get my baby out of that bed, come on home." I just watched as the tears streamed down his face. I packed up and left the motel with him and returned to our house. He found me through our caller ID. The cab driver called me when he arrived to pick me up. Mike and I continued to play cat and mouse. The phrase "I'm sorry and I love you" meant nothing. I didn't love myself, so there was no way that Mike loved me. Emotionally I was a wreck. I didn't have many people to talk to. I felt embarrassed. Everyone loved Mike, so who was I to take that image away from them. However, after being on a conference call with classmates from my biology class I went upstairs to take a shower and go to bed. Here comes Mike "who was that guy on the phone?" I said "what are you talking about?" Mike continued to yell in my face and grab me by the arms. The guy on the call was another classmate. Apparently, Mike was listening to the conference call. So, forget that he heard all the content of the conversation. That didn't matter because there was a man on the phone. And with that on the upcoming Friday I called my uncle with bags packed and I left for good while Mike was at work.

To think that I could rationalize with him was ridiculous. I was in so much pain. I couldn't see it while I was living in it. I cried and I asked myself over and over again why? What was it about me that was so unlovable? It wasn't that I was unlovable. The problem was that I did not love myself. I was in a pattern of attracting brokenness because I wasn't pouring into myself what I was giving to others.

From that phase of brokenness within my marriage I

became intentional about my mission to transform the way

that I approached love and self-care. As I tuned into myself

in a deep intimate way by giving myself permission to take

care of me. Through the process of self-love and

nurturance, my journey involved spending time with myself

asking tough questions like: "What is it that I need, how

can I give it to myself first, who am I, what do I deserve;

and what do I want my life to look and feel like?"

Everything that I said that I wanted, deserved and needed, I

began to give it to myself on an emotional, spiritual,

psychological and social level. This created the foundation

for what is known as internal happiness. I felt a sense of

peace that I did not want to let go of. Taking ownership of

my well-being, shifted me into a space of worthiness. From

that point I learned what it really meant to feel complete

and to be whole.

A Quest to Feel Wanted

Chasity Chandler

"Those who have a strong sense of love and belonging have the courage to be imperfect."

-Dr. Brené Brown

They say that little girls learn how to love and be loved based on their relationship with their father. What happens to that girl's perspective, road map to love or relationships when she doesn't have a healthy male role model to guide her? I can't speak for all those little girls, but I can speak for myself and how I interpret life's journey in the realm of love, life and relationships. In this chapter I intend to give you an in-depth look at my journey to wholeness and my quest for whole-hearted living.

The beginning was just me, my mom and my dad. I'm not sure how things were before they broke-up, but I've heard the stories and seems as though that was what was best at that time. I hear that I was a daddy's little girl and being as though I was his only child, I presume I was. As I grew older the tone was set to be showered with false-promises, late cancellations/no shows, months of no contact, that lead to years of silence. If the first man that is supposed to love you and show you how you are supposed to be treated lies, lets you down and disappears with no communication for years at a time one might search for that love and belonging in other places, people or things. I'm not done with the impacts of my relationships and life as it

 relates to my father, but I will circle back to that later in this chapter. Needless to say, I didn't know that this would set the tone for thirty-four years of yearning to be wanted, searching for love in the wrong places with people who were incapable of loving me the way I deserved.

My first sexual encounter was not one of butterflies and rainbows. It was a slow eradication of truth, innocence and affirmed that sometimes even the good men or boys are deceitful and have ulterior motives. Don't get me wrong, I'm not putting all men in one basket or making a generalization based on societal norms. I'm simply saying that everything that glitters ain't gold and just because it looks good or feels good doesn't mean that it is good for you. That experience unfortunately happened more than once. The violation of my flesh by someone I trusted, someone who was supposed to protect me, someone that I felt cared about me and me about them became a semi-normal occurrence. One that would eventually instill deep feelings of self-doubt, low self-worth, shame and a whole lot a guilt for a 7-year-old to bare alone for over two decades.

This led to falling for the bull-headed, playboy, sweet talking, charming and sometimes fine ass types time and time again. When I was in the thick of things and experiencing what I thought was love and being "in love" I was blind to the way I was accepting subpar treatment, requesting less and giving more. It wasn't a lot of men or boyfriends, but it was enough to teach me some valuable lessons. The relationship that has shaped or impacted me most is that of my first real love. The man that shared my heart, my life, planted the seed for my children, my everything. He was the person I thought that I would get to live out my happily ever after with, boy was I wrong!

He wasn't the normal type of guy I'd go for, other than the fact that he played sports, but his persistence really intrigued me. I remember seeing him around, at the park, at the local community center and eventually grad bash during my junior year when I accompanied my best friend at the time in celebration of her senior year. The craziest part of all is I remember hearing him say "I'm going to marry her" to his cousin and I would laugh and think "Dude, you're not even my type". Well that changed after long night talks outside my window that were covered by burglar bars and the passing of notes that completely spoke to my heart.

All the sweet nothings and heartfelt words and gestures led me to falling deeply in love and making myself extremely susceptible to things that would eventually lead to me becoming a pregnant senior in high school and giving birth to our first daughter just four months after graduation and three months after my eighteenth birthday. A shocking truth that would rock my world as my heart was set on going to college in Tallahassee to play basketball and pursue my degree in psychology. After all, I had busted my ass to get high test scores to play division one ball and go after my dream of becoming a lawyer. My path was now on a detour.

My dream to attend college did not stop there. When my daughter was three months old I started my associate's degree in psychology at the local community college. Me and the love of my life lived in my mother's home for a few months as we saved for a place of our own. The following year during Christmas the young man that had won my heart and gifted me with my first born dropped to one knee in front of his paternal side of the family and asked me to be his wife and spend the rest of our lives together. I weep in pure joy and shock and gave a sounding "Yes". Everyone cheered us on and congratulated us.

It appeared life was beginning to look up and love was really going to suit me. We continued to work on the relationship and doing what we thought was best to have a strong marriage. I never really knew what a healthy, strong and loving relationship looked like. I grew up in a single parent home in a very small town and no real examples of a marriage. My grandmother had a long-term boyfriend and always said "I'm so set in my ways; I'm not changing for nobody". When she found out he was cheating she kicked him out and didn't think twice. That was over twenty years ago, and she is still single. I guess she meant what she said! My husband at the time's family had a very different history. His grand-parents had been married over forty years at the time and his parents, despite their ups and downs were still married and had been for over twenty years. The list of relatives went on and on. The expectations for our union was forever, as that's how it worked in their world. On June 18, 2005 we began that journey. Just three days after my twenty-first birthday. My mother invited my father to the wedding. I hadn't spoken to him in years. It turns out that being absent from your daughter's life does not lend for regular phone calls or meetups for brunch. He was happy to be there for the rehearsal dinner and wanted to make sure that I was sure that I wanted to go through with the wedding. He even asked me if I was going to hyphenate my last name. I still remember the look on his face when I told him I wasn't. I was torn as to whether I was going to allow him the honor of walking me down the aisle or my mother's father. The next day I said I do in front of friends, family, my love and God. That was one of the happiest days of my life. I came down the aisle so fast people thought I was running. I escorted myself. That day my husband shed tears when he watched me make my way down in my beautiful strapless, ivory form fighting gown covered in Swarovski crystals and an amazing train that would later have a wonderful French bustle. From there we went on to honeymoon in the Bahamas for five nights and six days that were amazing. It seems like yesterday I was given the Jamie Foxx CD for Christmas and we were trying to conceive our first child as a married couple. At this point I had already graduated from the local community college and was well into my bachelor's degree in psychology at a larger university and now in pursuit of my dreams of being a Clinical Psychologist. Yes, that's different from my original goal of being a lawyer. Let's just say I was always going to be a psychology major but watching my family-in-law go through a life changing tragedy and loss of a young family member made me feel like I would be of better use as a helper as opposed to a lawyer. We found out we were expecting our second child and were excited to meet her.

She was born, in all her perfection, named after her cousin who had passed away in that life changing tragedy.

Life was good. We had the occasional argument or disagreement, but things hadn't gotten bad. They eventually would. To the point that we had several separations for up to a year each, relations with others during that time, a restraining order following an arrest for domestic violence and more.

The day after I was tossed around like a rag doll, in the presence of our sleeping daughters due to receiving a phone call from someone I had agreed not to communicate with after we had gotten back together. According to the dude it was a pure accident, but led to the destruction of my lamp, a huge punched hole through my headboard, being chocked and so much more. That night the police were called and due to this man, you know the one I loved who was my everything, who I had grown up with lied. Tried to claim I was the aggressor and due to his size compared to mine, both of us were about to be arrested for domestic violence. They kept us separated during the interview process like on television. As a desperate attempt to keep our children out of state custody I called our neighbor, who was his female friend and later I'd discover lover to see if she was in route to home and he called his parents to see if they could come from the other side of town. Neither got there in time enough and the police grew impatient and my husband was placed in cuffs. He heard my plea for him to be honest and how this lie would Impact our children and ruin my career. I was an ESE teacher for autistic children with varying exceptionality at the time and completing my master's degree in Professional Mental Health Counseling. He told the truth and was taken away right as his parents parked and watched him enter the police vehicle. Up to this point I felt like I couldn't eat, sleep or breathe without him. This was the true start to my journey of re-discovering who I was and the potential I had inside. The quiet after the storm was the worse. My sister came over to assist and console me, but I just couldn't stop thinking about what had just happened and how that was going to impact my life moving forward. How can the man that I felt was my everything treat me like I was nothing more than some bitch off the street? This isn't how God intended marriage to be and how would I be able to look my kids in the face again if I went back? These were the questions that I asked myself. I didn't have the answers, but I knew that better was going to come because I couldn't get much lower than this.

I got up the next day and went to the court house and got a restraining order. I also turned in his guns to the sheriff office instead of his parents. Yes, I was fearful for my life and had no idea what he would be capable of when he was released. After speaking with the sheriff who took my report, he commended me for taking this step to protect myself and not putting up with the bullshit anymore. Deep down inside I was proud of myself as well.

What I learned over that next almost two years was that the heart can change, forgiveness can take place and a relationship can still not work out. The fact that I would not only breathe, eat and sleep without my husband, but I could soar. I was worthy of love and more than enough for any suitable partner. My husband's lack of faithfulness and need to feel that he "still had it" had brought back those feelings and insecurities of that 7-year-old girl that's innocence had been stolen. I did what most people do and that's turn to what I knew best, my faith, and went full force into school, work and raising my kids. During that time, I re-dedicated my life to Christ and worked at really being a better person on every level. As a result of doing this I felt convicted to give my marriage another shot. As I felt that was the right thing to do. After a year of being separated we got back together and two months later I was pregnant with our only son. Fast forward a year, I took my then three children to see my father since I hadn't seen him since my wedding, five years prior. That was the first time he had seen two of the three grandchildren. Little did I know that would be the last time I'd see him alive. Five months later he was dead, and it had been ruled a suicide. Just four months after I asked my husband for a divorce and five months after my grandmother had passed away. This was the straw that caused me to drop out of my doctorate program, well this and my computer dying. Now I was fatherless, separated and torn as to what I would do. Seemed like a fucked-up situation to be in. I had already obtained my master's degree and was now living alone with my children and my mother. Starting all over, losing the only family that I really had left, which was his. I was able to push through in the same area for about another three or four years. Then I was given an offer for a ten-thousand-dollar increase with a chance to relocate and I took it. I looked at the things that had gone wrong in my life, a chance for me and my kids to start over and that's what I did.

Moving to an area where you know NO ONE can be a lonely and scary place. Taking the bull by the horns was the only way I knew how to be strong amid that level of discomfort. I couldn't allow things to crumble, as failure was not an option. Fast forward four years and now I have a thriving private practice in three different locations, 20 contractors, I'm a published author and in the process of launching three new businesses, one of which will change the face of how people of color view becoming a certified sex therapist and make a clear message that there is no ceiling that cannot be broken. I share this not to boast, but to leave a legacy for my three children that shows them no matter where you come from, what happens to you and how many times you screw up in life...... you can still win. This journey has not been easy and it sure as hell hasn't been all fun and games, but what I can say without a shadow of a doubt is that the woman, mother, daughter, sister, friend, boss, business partner, entrepreneur, girlfriend and someday future wife that I am is thankful for all the heartache, abuse, lies, backstabbing, prejudice and overlooking that I've endured over the last thirty-four years and it has been more than worth it! I cannot change what I've been through, not even how it has impacted me, but I can take back my power and learn how to re-write my story. I'm a survivor, not a victim and I have dedicated the remainder of my life providing services and empowerment to those who have yet to find their voice, couples who want to have happier, healthier and stronger relationships or those who want to be authentically themselves no matter who in the hell doesn't like it! Shame and guilt are just as rampant as STIs and bad tweets. Don't allow it to steal your thunder. The quest to feel wanted is simply the ability to accept who you are in all your imperfections and learn to live wholeheartedly despite the risk because the reward will

be amazing.

Unapologetically Me

Chautè Thompson

"I must feel safe and protected in my relationship before I am vulnerable with my partner" these are the words that resonated with me as I had a conversation with a few girlfriends. When is the last time you felt secure and protected? We as women desire to feel secure and protected in a relationship but how often do we REALLY feel this way? Can you recall the last time you felt Secure and Protected at the same time? For me the last time I felt secure and protected was 2007. I remember because this is the year I was pregnant with my youngest. This is when I started the process of fighting for my marriage, since then it spiraled downward into me losing myself and accepting less than I deserved.

"Hey Tay, the guys are taking a trip to Dominican Republic and I want to go, it's for a few days and we are staying in a villa" were his words to me. "Go, have fun," I said. Pregnant with his youngest, I thought nothing of a "guy's trip", but this started the process I did not foresee. As he returned I felt a difference and when I got the courage to address it, it was quickly dismissed. As I started to listen to my gut- this gift given to me from above, I snooped and found pictures which raised concern. Being creative and finding ways to force the truth out was unsuccessful, it only built mistrust and distance between us when we were already growing apart. I started this internal battle with myself and God. Reading books, journaling, being positive, doing my best to be the perfect wife, making sure I do nothing to stress him out or make him upset. The happy days were still not enough as his trips moved from two a year with the guys to four trips, two with the guys and two alone. Every year he felt more at peace in a country which wasn't home.

Birthdays were forgotten, there was no special day in our relationship and every day was approached as just another day. My words meant nothing, my feelings not validated. I was insecure in a marriage which was supposed to be my haven. I did not feel protected; the best friend I married felt like a stranger.

I despise the silent treatment. In all relationships communication is vital. It was the norm in my home to get the silent treatment if my husband was unhappy with something. The silence that hurt the most was him not being happy with the way I decided to allocate money to pay my tithes, this caused a rift in our relationship which brought about a two-week silent treatment. During this time his parents were visiting with us, for two weeks his parents witnessed my husband not talk to me and not even looking my way. "You know what pisses me off, don't piss me off." Silent treatment ended!

He stopped complimenting me. He found my size six to be unattractive. He felt like my confidence deteriorated due to the lack of affirmations I received from him. He did not consider the mistrust he created. With all this, he was adamant that he NEVER cheated. We all have a breaking point. Mine were the endless letters I wrote to him. The pleas and begging him to hear my heart. The requests to stop traveling to a place that brought insecurity in our relationship. It was the unreciprocated requests I made for us to date again. To build a friendship that was stronger than the first. Taking the time to evolve together…All were turned down. It was the living like roommates. It was the desire for my baby girls to see their mother treated like a queen, so one day they would know to accept NOTHING LESS! My last plea was in February 2014. I asked him to forgo his scheduled trip. I guessed my feelings of not being comfortable with the trip were not enough. "It's your problem, deal with it" were his words. Those words helped me to realize that I was not valued, my feelings were not enough, our relationship did not matter enough, and the fight left me.

I was preparing for work and also getting the kids their dinner before dropping them off at the babysitter. There was a knock at the door. I was a little confused, as I was not expecting anyone. I opened the door I see a man dressed in a white collared polo and dress pants with a badge, to my surprise I was being served. After this emotional experience I still needed to work and show face for my children. This began a cycle of difficult nights ahead. "I'm only giving you want you want", he eventually said to me. *He still didn't get it...* I wanted him to love me, date me, take the time to know me, listen to my heart, value my feelings. I wanted our marriage to work and for the needed effort to be put into it. However, if he wasn't going to try and if he wasn't going to value me as his wife, I *can* do *bad* by myself.

Years later, I wished him well as my children have traveled to his most traveled destination and is developing a relationship with his Dominican fiancée.

Dating has been a journey, with so many stories! This journey is a new one for two reasons. First, I never dated before marrying my husband. Second, so many years have passed, times have surely changed! Throughout this journey of meeting individuals, the protection and security I desire still has not presented itself yet. Let me share a taste of my dating journey.

"I could snap your neck before anyone can come to save you", were the words Travis said to me. The look in his eyes spoke to me. He was not himself. With his military background I knew he could make good on his threat. Scared for my life I locked myself in the bathroom. These moments were not the bulk of our interaction but when they occurred it scared the bejesus out of me! Secure and protected? Oddly, I felt at peace with him when he was himself, but alcohol changed him. I thought my boundaries were enough to keep me safe. There were at least four instances which I was scared for my life, none as bad as the one described but why remain in a situation filled with uncertainty, insecurity and no protection?

Online dating welcomed a new fold into my life. This one was a motivational speaker or, so Malcolm shared with me, but he was learning the ropes- we all must start somewhere. When we discussed future, I shared a desire of wanting to be with someone who will ease my load of working overtime for my family. His response left me confused. "We can struggle together", he said. This is totally not what secure and protected looks like to me.

Then there was Avery, who experienced one trauma after the other. No one can understand the rollercoaster of emotions it is to watch someone you care about dearly break apart in front of your eyes. It sucks the life out of you. I was pleading for him not to take his own life while also pleading for him to allow me to save his kids' life. The battle within me was strong, not wanting to betray him by involving law enforcement and knowing I needed to involve them. My heart was breaking. I was *mentally*, *physically*, and *emotionally* drained.

Now, let's discuss Cedric. He sweet talked me, made me feel desired and adored. "Every girl deserves a guy that can make her heart forget that it was ever broken" he sent me a meme by curiano.com with this quote, it spoke life, have I found this one? It felt like it, but it was short lived, he made me feel this way for a brief second, until he gave me the silent treatment, which came after numerous inconsistencies of being able to keep his word. I did not feel like I was forgetting my heart was ever broken, instead I was discovering how much he reminded me of when my heart was broken.

In addition to experiencing these interactions during my dating years I also shared beautiful moments with guys who did an excellent job of giving me the illusion of a relationship. These moments were filled with creating memories, great conversations, companionship, happiness and everything a real relationship entails but it was lacking

the commitment. We had an understanding that they were

emotionally unable or probably a more fitting word is

unwilling to commit to me due to their own life experiences

which caused trepidation to move in the direction of

commitment. The illusion is what I call it and what I chose

to accept repeatedly. This one was one of the hardest

because my heart gets wrapped up in it. I allow myself to

forget that it's an illusion because it feels so real, but the

fact ALWAYS remains- I have absolutely no security and

protection in the illusion painted before me.

If I didn't define myself for myself, I would be crunched into
other people's fantasies for me and eaten alive.
                                                                    -Audre Lorde

Becoming unapologetically me took stages of growth. It's

been a process for me, from marrying the person I deemed

my best friend to fighting for my marriage and losing

myself in the process. I was scared to speak on topics that

raised concerns for me, things I was unhappy with or

simply wanted to gain clarity on because I did not want to risk my husband threatening to leave me and making good on his threat. It continued with the process of finding myself, my voice, my worth and journeying to love me so much that the opinions of others didn't have as much value. This process took years, I made strides then became stagnant and this was a cycle until I was divorced.

Although I am a witness that the statistics are correct when it says divorce is the second most traumatic event one can experience next to death of a loved one, I can honestly say the growth I have endured after my relationship ended is one of the positives from my divorce. I am a Whole New Me and I can contribute this to the reflecting and processing I did throughout my journey. I experienced 5 stages in my growth.

First, I went through the stages of grief to finally accepting being single. There have been numerous triggers to sadness and moments of feeling lonely. I worked daily taking care of everyone else's problems and came home to an empty home some nights with no energy or motivation to do anything other than wrapping up under my blanket, numb to the world. I moved from being lonely to loving my own company. Second, mindset shift. Perspective can make you or break you, this showed itself to be true for me as I reflected on my experiences and committed to looking at the glass half full. When I did this even my worst days were good days. Third, I learned the lesson of forgiveness. I was already a very forgiving person, but I challenged myself to forgive someone who never apologized. I found ways to be thankful for the lessons I learned instead of being bitter that I experienced them. After I made these decisions the magic started to happen. I was able to rewrite my story with a new ending. I was able to turn the page and not be defined by my marriage ending.

Fourth, I set new goals, new boundaries, I developed my deal breakers and I consumed my presence with affirmations. I started to KNOW my WORTH! I embraced that although I am not perfect I am beautiful in the skin I'm in. I am perfectly imperfect and whoever enters my life will accept me, embrace this truth and appreciate me for who I am. I will have the opportunity to accept someone else's perfect imperfections and together we will complement each other, not complete each other.

Fifth, this journey also taught me to ask for help. I wear so many hats, taking care of so many individuals and tending to the needs and desires of others that it becomes easy to continue down the path of forgetting myself. During my process of healing I realized depression and burnout are two outcomes which can occur if I did not take breaks, ask for help and have/utilize my support system.

Living unapologetically, I have grown to a place of wanting companionship but needing my personal time to enjoy my own company. I am now able to appreciate my flaws and make continual strides to better myself as an individual. I am less concerned with the noise around me of others' perceptions of me instead I look in the mirror and the rearview mirror reflecting on decisions I've made and embracing the journey I am on. Self-discovery has been an amazing experience with highs and lows, adventures, questions, research, naivety and lessons learned. Living unapologetically is not an obnoxious way of living, its empowering, it's embracing who I am at the core and being assertive enough to live authentically in my truth. I am a Whole New Me, a Brand New Me!

As You Journey

Sometimes as we journey we forget our value. We get so caught up in tending to others that we accept the treatment others give, ignoring that we deserve so much more. We lose sight of our dreams. The light that once shone so brightly starts to dim. Though the paths we take have mountains and valleys filled with doubts and worries, shame and frustration, we have to learn to take a stand. Focus on our own growth. Here's an affirmation for you or create your own:

I am loved. I am beautiful. I am worthy of so much more.

I am ENOUGH!

Treading along on our journey dreaming of our own happily ever after discouraged as we are happy for others but dreading our own desires of companionship not being fulfilled, losing hope becomes easy. Unsuccessful Relationship after unsuccessful relationship, we are here to remind you that Your Happily Ever After can still occur!

Do the work on you, live wholeheartedly, develop your deal breakers, open yourself to the possibilities, allow yourself to be vulnerable with individuals who earn your trust, remember that a relationship is a risk- be open to the risk and be intentional. Your Happily Ever After is not a fairytale.

With free will we can learn from our own life experiences and/or from the experiences of others. As time passes we see more and more that history repeats itself. Knowing this affords you the opportunity to use the stories in this book to:

1. Know that you are not alone on your journey.
2. Remember that life experiences are our teachers.
3. Embrace your journey for what it is and boldly press forward empowered to do what's necessary to be free to LIVE.

Love starts within. Many times, we desire someone else to love us but to be whole we must first love ourselves. Is there something prohibiting you from loving you? Take a moment to list the numerous things you love about yourself, list why you are worthy of love, list what you bring to the relationship (romantic, familial, and friendships), list the boundaries and deal breakers you will implement because you love you. When you love you enough to accept nothing less than you deserve this energy will exude from your pores and you will attract others in your life that will appreciate you loving you and you being open to love others.

Past encounters have the ability to shape how we perceive ourselves as well as what we expect and accept from others. We each have the power regardless of our educational backgrounds to push forward with self-determination and motivation to be more and do more. The quest to feel wanted starts with embracing the perfectly imperfect you and authentically living wholeheartedly. As you journey to pursue wholeness you will experience pain but allow the bumps in the road to motivate you to live unapologetically you. Embrace your flaws and do the work of self-improvement in whichever ways you deem necessary or desired. Venture out to try new things, learn new likes and rekindle old likes. Enjoy your own company, live life with an attitude of gratitude, forgive for the wrongs done against you without the apology, let life be your lifelong classroom teaching you lessons, Rewrite your story.

Journeying from pain to greatness is no easy task. Be gracious with yourself. Take the time to realize that you are enough, love yourself unconditionally, embrace your journey as your teacher and live free, embracing your authentic self, start your quest to feel wanted with the internal work of wholeheartedly be unapologetically you and live out your happily ever after.

CONTRIBUTING AUTHORS

Chanel Spencer

Chanel, a New York City native, is the CEO and Founder of Maximum Evolution. She is a dynamic motivational speaker, writer, and executive coach with a powerful story of overcoming adversity. As a mother with young children, Chanel has worked her way up the corporate ladder to become a General Manager and continues to develop her professional career while mentoring others to do the same. Chanel has developed a dynamic mentorship program designed to help you discover your path while setting realistic goals to move you forward, teaching you tools to navigate through personal and professional obstacles. Chanel works with people one on one empowering them to *maximize constantly and evolve instantly.* She is currently writing a memoir and developing an online course set to be released early 2019.

To learn more or to contact Ms. Spencer:

www.maxevol.com
info@maxevol.com

LaQuista Erinna, LCSW

LaQuista Erinna is an Army Veteran with over 19 years of service. After returning home from her second deployment to Iraq, she became increasingly concerned with the challenges service members faced upon reintegration into civilian lives. She realized that she wanted to help people live their best lives. She decided to pursue a Masters of Social Work degree with a specialization in Health and Military Social Work, from the University of Southern California. Currently, LaQuista is finalizing the degree requirements for a Doctorate of Behavioral Health through Arizona State University.

LaQuista spent years providing homeless veterans outreach and intensive case management with the federal government. Wanting to provide more direct clinical services, she decided to open her own private practice. As a licensed clinical social worker, LaQuista is trained to treat numerous issues ranging from stress management to more serious mental illnesses. She specializes in helping people cope with depression, anxiety, trauma, and PTSD. Today, LaQuista helps individuals, couples, and families to heal from past traumas as well as current issues that may be affecting their lives. She continues to be an advocate for some of the most vulnerable populations and volunteers regularly with several non-profit organizations in her community. She is also an author, speaker, and consultant for medical providers who wish to integrate behavioral health care into their practices.

To learn more or to contact Ms. Erinna:

www.laquistaerinna.com
info@laquistaerinna.com

Andrea Stuckey

Andrea M. Stuckey is passionate about helping women through the devastating life changes that come with separation and divorce. She is the Founder of Live Life Luvd Coaching LLC where she is dedicated to helping women rebuild their lives through transformational life coaching, speaking, teaching and writing. She is the author of "Suddenly Single: A Woman's Spiritual and Practical Guide to the First Five Years Following Separation and Divorce", "Picking Up the Pieces After Divorce", and "Liberation Journal for Divorcées: 90 Days to Renewing Your Personal Freedom." She teaches women how to cultivate and activate their gifts and talents, in order to redefine their lives and pursue their dreams. Having gone through divorce twice, she empowers women, shares her journey, and gives spiritual and practical tips that are applicable to live a liberated lifestyle.

To learn more or to contact Ms. Stuckey:

www.livelifeluvd.com
andrea@livelifeluvd.com

Rashida Ingram, MS, MFT

Rashida is a Certified Marriage & Family Therapist and PhD student specializing in assisting individuals and couples to make sense of their life's purpose during times of transition, grief, separation or family discord. Rashida began to make her mark as an Innergy Empowerment Specialist in 2011 after graduating from Capella University with a Master of Science degree in Marriage and Family Therapy. Rashida is also an undergraduate of Temple University, where she received her Bachelor of Arts degree in Psychology (2000). She is a solution-focused energy based specialist with a mindful approach that encourages clients to think critically and compassionately about themselves; as they successfully navigate their life process. From the philosophy of "Create the life you've imagined, so that you can lead the life you love," Rashida manifested her own counseling practice in 2012. Innergy Connections, LLC Empowerment for Authentic Living & Mindful Connections was established to broaden the scope of our connections and intimate partnerships to include authentic methods of engagement, cultivate growth and inspire action. All of which creates opportunities for healing, and transformation. Through teaching, coaching and self-reflection, individuals and families learn to understand the creative force of their Innergy and ways to leverage it as a tool to manifest their best life instead of existing in best case circumstances. Rashida continues to engage underrepresented groups who traditionally reject therapy as a viable option to improving their way of being in the world. In addition to Innergy Connections, Rashida has taken notice of the adverse effects of trauma, poor social connections and touch deprivation. She has begun to facilitate what is now known as touch positive support therapy and cuddle workshops. These workshops assist participants to heal the disconnection between avoidance and secure attachment. She currently lives in Philadelphia, Pennsylvania.

To learn more or to contact Ms. Ingram:

www.innergyconnectionstherapy.com
rashida@innergyconnectionstherapy.com

Chasity Chandler, LMHC, MCAP, ICADC, CST, CDWF

Chasity Chandler is a Licensed Mental Health Counselor, Masters level Certified Addictions Professional, Internationally Certified Alcohol and Drug Counselor, Certified Sex Therapist EMDR trained clinician, Certified Daring Way Facilitator, Qualified Supervisor for Mental Health Counselors and soon for Marriage and Family Therapists. She is also a Certified Prepare Enrich facilitator for dating, marital and pre-marital couples. Chasity is the CEO of Center for Sexual Health & Wellness, LLC. Chasity has earned her Associate's & Bachelor's Degrees in Psychology and her Master's Degree in Counseling with an Emphasis in Professional Mental Health Counseling. Chasity is currently pursuing additional certifications in Substance Abuse and Sex Education. Chasity is a professional Member of (AASECT), American Association of Sexuality Educators, Counselors.

Chasity has over 16 years of experience in the helping field. She specializes in working with children, teenagers, adults on general mental health, trauma, sex/sexuality issues and substance abuse. She works extensively with the LGBTQ+ population on and not limited the following areas: general therapy around daily concerns, coming out, gender therapy, hRt consideration and letters, support with family/partners, advocacy and more. She does a lot of work with couples on areas of communication, conflict resolution, increase intimacy and passion in their relationship as well as infidelity and more.

In addition to counseling, Chasity is a speaker, published author, trainer and offers coaching, consultation and supervision to other professionals and entrepreneurs. She provides authenticity coaching and is a Certified Daring Way Facilitator; experiential methodology based on the research of Dr. Brené Brown.

To learn more about Chasity Chandler visit her at:

www.centerforsexualhealthandwellness.com
Chasity@centerforsexualhealthandwellness.com

Or, on Social Media:

IG: https://www.instagram.com/chasforchange
FB: https://www.facebook.com/catalystforchange2016/
LinkedIn: https://www.linkedin.com/in/chasforchange
Twitter: https://www.twitter.com/chasforchange

ABOUT THE AUTHOR

Chautè Thompson. LMHC, CDWF

Chautè Thompson, LMHC, is a speaker, author, consultant, educator, transformation coach, certified family mediator and qualified parenting coordinator. She offers life changing strategies, empowerment, personal development, mental and emotional health messages to schools, churches, conferences, workshops and retreats. She is passionate about helping others grow mentally, emotionally and spiritually into the best version of themselves.

Ms. Thompson is the owner of Inspiring Hope Counseling Services, LLC (IHCS) a private practice in Florida which focuses on helping all families strengthen their family unit helping them to become healthier and happier, specializing in working with families of divorce to transition smoothly. IHCS also specializes in women's issues, transitions, parenting support, helping individuals and families work through self-discovery, anxiety, depression, behavioral problems, anger management, and PTSD. She provides Christian Counseling in addition to counseling for the deaf and hard of hearing.

Ms. Thompson is also the founder of Brand New Me, LLC (BNM). BNM focuses on providing resources, coaching, education and empowerment enabling women to rediscover and redefine themselves growing past the pain of divorce and other life changing events, enabling wholeheartedness.

To learn more or connect with Ms. Thompson

www.inspirehopehealthhealing.com
www.brandnewmejourney.com
info@chautethompson.com

www.instagram.com/chautethompson
www.facebook.com/thetransformationadvocate
www.facebook.com/brandnewmejourney

CPSIA information can be obtained
at www.ICGtesting.com
Printed in the USA
FSHW022243130219
55601FS